The Secret of the Robo-Reindeer

A Christmas Adventure

Sebastian D. Torell

No robots were harmed in the creation of this product.

Copyright © 2023

Contact the author:
www.noah-leon.com

Illustrations by Claudio Eumir Sepúlveda
Contact the illustrator:
Instagram: @claudioeumir,
Facebook: claudio.sepulveda.50

Cover illustration coloring by Jesús Ramón Camberos

All rights reserved.

ISBN: 9798865069188

For Sebastian and Simon

CONTENTS

1 A CHILLING ENCOUNTER 7
2 THE FROSTBITE LEGEND 11
3 GONE 15
4 MYSTERIOUS PURSUERS 17
5 THE REFLECTION 21
6 INGENIOUS CONSTRUCTORS 25
7 THE GREAT SLEIGH ESCAPE 29
8 MRS. SMITH 33
9 INTERROGATION AT THE CHRISTMAS MARKET 37
10 THE CONNECTION TO THE NORTH POLE 41
11 ALLURING TOYS 43
12 SANTA'S REAL JOB 47
13 THE SECRET CHIP 51
14 A PLAN TAKES SHAPE 55
15 THE DECOY REINDEER 57
16 MIDNIGHT 59
17 MOONLIGHT CHASE 63
18 AN INVITATION FROM THE NORTH 67
19 THE ROBOTICS FACTORY 69

20	WHISPERS IN THE WIND	73
21	BENEATH THE TRAPDOOR	77
22	THE TRUE FACE	81
23	THE ROBOT ARMY	85
24	THE FROSTENBITT MOMENT	89
	EPILOGUE: A CHRISTMAS TO REMEMBER	93

1
A CHILLING ENCOUNTER

It was the holiday season, and the whole town dazzled with twinkling lights. Joyful carols and the familiar scents of Christmas filled the crisp atmosphere.

The long-awaited day of the Christmas market's grand opening had come.

Leon adjusted his favourite scarf, its wool tickling his neck. He had been bouncing up and down with excitement all day. "Do you think the new reindeer is cooler than the old one?" he asked Noah, his best friend.

"Guess we'll know in a minute," Noah said as they headed toward the marketplace. "But honestly, I don't get why they'd switch out the old plastic reindeer. That was, like, the symbol of the market."

Soon, they found themselves in the middle of the action. Booths overflowed with trinkets and treats. Laughter and cheer filled the air, and the aroma of roasted almonds and spiced cider surrounded them.

And then they saw the new Robo-Reindeer. Even from a distance, they noticed that it had bright blue eyes. It moved up and down gracefully, decked out in lights and ribbons.

"How awesome is that!" Leon exclaimed. He dashed toward the mechanical marvel, and Noah followed suit.

But in their rush, they collided with a shadowy figure.

"Ouch!" Noah found himself on the ground, rubbing his forehead.

Two mysterious eyes peered out from under a dark hood. For a moment they met Noah's gaze and sent a chill down his spine. "Sorry," mumbled the figure, the words tinged with a foreign accent, before disappearing into the crowd.

"Look what he dropped!" Leon picked up a flyer from the ground. "*The Gift Your Child Really Wants!*" he read out loud.

"A toy ad?" Noah raised an eyebrow.

"Boring!" Leon declared, tossing the flyer aside.

"Let's go check out that reindeer up close," Noah suggested.

The Robo-Reindeer looked as if it had just landed from the future via a time machine.

"Wow, it's glowing blue now!" Leon exclaimed, fascinated by the fur, which kept subtly changing its colour.

"Yeah, and look at its eyes!" Noah added. "They're not just bright blue; there's something almost intelligent about them."

The mechanical creature paced back and forth. Every so often, it would puff out steam from its nostrils like a mini locomotive.

"Check this out, Leon!" Noah pulled out his phone and showed a picture from last year.

"Compared to this one, the old reindeer looks like it's straight out of the Stone Age," Leon remarked. With that, he tapped the reindeer on its nose.

The response was a mechanical snort. Both boys burst into laughter.

"I am wondering how something like this ends up at a small Christmas market like ours?" Noah pondered. "This thing must've cost a fortune."

Just then, Leon tugged at Noah's jacket. "There! It's that guy from earlier!"

Noah followed Leon's pointing finger, spotting the dark-clad figure lurking in the shadows. He jolted as their eyes met again.

Without a second thought, the two friends sprinted toward the mysterious figure. The stranger, sensing their pursuit, picked up his pace, skillfully weaving through booths and the throng of people.

The boys tried to keep up, dodging past families and swerving around stands. The stranger seemed always just a step ahead, his silhouette occasionally obscured by the crowds.

As they neared the market's edge, the figure vanished into the dimly lit streets and passages of the city. Noah and Leon skidded to a halt, scanning the vicinity. Before them stretched a maze of paths and shadows.

"Where'd he go?" Leon asked, frustration etched on his face.

A loud crash echoed from one of the alleys.

The boys locked eyes. Then, as if propelled by the same burst of adrenaline, they bolted toward the source of the sound.

2
THE FROSTBITE LEGEND

Noah and Leon raced into the alley where the hooded figure was about to regain his footing. It seemed he had slipped on the icy ground and crashed into a garbage can.

Before the boys could react, a stern voice boomed behind them. "Hey, what are you kids doing here?"

They spun around to find a burly security guard eyeing them suspiciously.

"Help us, quick!" Leon shouted. "We need to interrogate that suspect!" He gestured behind him, but when he looked back, the figure had vanished, as if swallowed by the earth.

"All I see here is a knocked-over trash can. Did you guys do that?" the guard inquired.

"No, we didn't," Noah assured him.

The guard raised an eyebrow. "Oh, you didn't, eh? Maybe it was the ghost dog, Frostbite, pulling pranks again."

"Ghost dog? Frostbite?" Leon repeated, puzzled.

The guard leaned in, a playful glint in his eyes. "Don't you know?" His voice dropped to a whisper.

"In winter's chill, at day or night,
Frostbite prowls, staying out of sight..."

He hesitated, his eyes shifting upwards as if trying to pull the remaining lines from the night sky. "Anyway! Frostbite is an age-old legend. They say he's a guardian spirit that occasionally takes the form of a large dog."

Leon looked skeptical. "Really? Sounds more like bedtime stories to me."

"You know, legends often have a grain of truth in them", Noah chimed in. "Maybe Frostbite is real in some way."

The guard nodded solemnly. "It's said that for centuries he's been watching over this place, ensuring no harm comes to it." His expression softened. "Especially around Christmastime."

Noah glanced back to the spot where the figure had disappeared. "Maybe he can help us catch the suspect," he suggested with a mixture of doubt and hope in his voice.

The guard laughed heartily. "Well, good luck with that. But for now, back to the market you go." He wagged a finger at them. "And remember, better safe than sorry."

Feeling a bit disappointed that the hooded figure had slipped away, Noah and Leon trudged back to the market.

"This is all so weird," Noah mused, glancing at his phone. "Yikes, we should've been home ages ago!"

"Don't worry, we'll investigate more tomorrow," Leon assured him.

Just then, Leon's eyes caught something at one of the market stalls. "Wait up, I see something Mom would love. Give me a sec, will you?"

While Noah was waiting, he couldn't shake off the Frostbite

legend the guard had told them. Could there really be a guardian spirit watching over them? The thought was both comforting and eerie.

Leon returned, a satisfied smile on his face. "Got it. Mom's gonna love this."

"What did you get?" Noah asked.

"It's a surprise," Leon replied with a smirk. "Wasn't cheap, though," he added, slightly wincing. "But hey, it's for Mom. She deserves something special."

As they turned to leave, both threw a glance back at the Robo-Reindeer. Its glowing blue eyes seemed to be staring at them, filled with an inexplicable wisdom. As if it knew something they didn't.

3
GONE

As the sun rose, Noah and Leon were already up and about. The Robo-Reindeer and the mysterious hooded figure had filled their thoughts and kept them awake.

When the boys entered the market, most of the stalls were still covered with their protective tents, and a few vendors were beginning to set up.

When they approached the market's central square, they couldn't believe their eyes. Where the Robo-Reindeer had been the evening before was now only empty space. A few lights and ribbons lay scattered on the ground.

"It's just...gone?" Leon exclaimed in disbelief.

Noah scratched his head thoughtfully. "But how could this happen? Where could it have gone?"

They asked around, but everyone seemed clueless.

Leon threw his arms up in the air. "This is unbelievable!"

Noah pondered for a moment. "Maybe the market organizer knows something. Let's go talk to him."

The organizer's office was in a small cabin adorned with mistletoe and holly.

As they approached, they were greeted by a familiar face — the security guard from the day before. "You two again," he mumbled, winking at them. "Looking for Frostbite?"

"We're looking for the reindeer," Leon blurted out. "It's missing!"

The guard raised an eyebrow but said nothing. Just then, the cabin door opened, and out stepped Mr. Kruger, the market organizer. His expression was as frosty as the December weather.

"The reindeer was taken in for maintenance," he declared without a greeting.

"For maintenance?" Noah furrowed his brows. "It looked perfectly fine ye—"

"Enough with the questions," Mr. Kruger cut him off. "I'm sure you have other places to play."

As they left, they made their way down a narrow path lined with half-open booths. The smell of fresh coffee and cinnamon rolls began to fill the air.

"Don't you find this odd?", Leon whispered. His voice was almost drowned out by a nearby vendor unrolling a festive banner.

Noah stopped in front of a stall where a vendor was hanging glass ornaments, each one reflecting the morning sun. "Something's not right. The hooded guy, the missing reindeer, the strange behaviour of the organizer..."

"You think they're connected?" Leon asked.

"That's exactly what I'm thinking," Noah affirmed, his gaze lingering on a reindeer-shaped ornament. It seemed to catch the sun rays rather than reflect them. "And we need to get to the bottom of it."

4
MYSTERIOUS PURSUERS

Noah and Leon returned to the spot where the Robo-Reindeer had stood. With his keen eye for detail, Noah noticed something peculiar. "Look, Leon! There are hoofprints in the snow!"

Leon scratched his head. "How is that even possible? Did the reindeer go on a little adventure?" The thought of the Robo-Reindeer taking off on its own made him chuckle.

"We have to find out!" Noah declared resolutely.

They followed the hoofprints, which meandered through market stalls and rides, eventually leading onto a street. The trail continued through the winding alleys of the town center and headed toward the outskirts.

Finally, they arrived at the entrance of a forest, just as the rays of the morning sun began to illuminate the snow-covered path ahead.

The forest was quiet. Tall trees towered overhead, covered in frost. Damp earth and pine greeted their nostrils as birds chirped among the barren branches.

Noah grabbed Leon's arm and stopped. "Look up ahead!" he whispered, alarmed.

A pack of wild-looking dogs blocked the way. Their heads tilted curiously into the boys' direction and their eyes reflected the light in a mysterious glow.

"What are they up to?" Leon asked, taking a deep breath. "Are they … having a staring contest with us?"

Noah gulped. "I'm not sticking around to find out who blinks first. Let's back away slowly."

They began to retreat, but the dogs got up and began to trail them.

Both boys quickened their pace, their hearts racing. The dogs matched their speed, moving in eerie unison. The crunch of snow underfoot and the rhythmic panting of the dogs became a dance of pursuit.

The boys dashed deeper into the forest, breath misting in the chilly air.

Their escape route was blocked by a river. Glistening and calm, the water flowed along.

The dogs were almost upon them.

"What are we going to do, Noah?", Leon exclaimed, unease in his voice. "It's way too cold to jump in there!"

5
THE REFLECTION

Trying to calm his racing heart, Noah briefly turned his gaze to the serene river. His face, filled with unease, was reflected back to him from the water.

Yet behind his own reflection, he saw the trees and clouds merge, forming what looked to him like the silhouette of a friendly dog's face. The image wavered with each ripple, as if nodding in agreement. A flicker of sunlight danced across the water, making the silhouette appear to wink at him.

Leon noticed Noah's focus and whispered, "You're zoning out! What are you looking at?"

"I think... I saw Frostbite!" Noah exclaimed, his eyes wide with wonder.

Leon raised an eyebrow, "Seriously? In the water? You sure you didn't hit your head during our sprint?"

With newfound courage, Noah turned to face the dogs, who by now had formed a semi-circle around the boys. "I think they're just curious."

Leon looked skeptical. "Curious enough to have us for a snack?" Before Noah could answer, his face lit up. "Oh, now I know what got their attention. I forgot to take these out."

He reached into his pocket and pulled out a set of small, jingling Christmas bells. "Bought these for Mom on the Christmas market yesterday. She loves holiday decorations," he explained, shaking them gently. "And she's been working so hard lately, I thought a little holiday cheer could brighten up our place."

The tinkling sound seemed to enchant the dogs, their ears perking up, tails wagging. "Looks like we've got some fans," Leon grinned.

The dogs turned and began trotting away, pausing to look back as if to say, "Well, are you coming?"

Noah, still a bit dreamy, mused aloud, "Maybe Frostbite sent them to help us?"

Leon rolled his eyes, smirking, "Or maybe they just like these sounds. Either way, they seem to know where they're going."

The boys followed the dogs through the forest and before long, the familiar path with the reindeer's hoofprints came into view.

The dogs stopped, gazed at the boys for a moment, and then vanished into the woods, leaving Noah and Leon with a sense of wonder.

Leon shook his head in disbelief. "Well, that was unexpected."

Noah nodded, a twinkle in his eyes, "Unexpected, but we're back on track, quite literally."

They picked up the trail, which now led them uphill. The slope seemed endless and tested their endurance. Finally, the tracks led them to a hidden warehouse, nestled behind overgrown foliage.

They paused in front of the rusty warehouse door. "The hoofprints lead straight in," said Noah. "The reindeer is here, no doubt about it!"

Taking a deep breath, he reached for the doorknob. "Ready?"

Leon nodded. "Operation Reindeer Rescue is a go!"

The door creaked open with a sound that seemed to reverberate through the entire structure. Inside was dim, the only illumination coming from a lone bulb swaying overhead. A soft hum filled the space, broken only by the occasional drip of water.

With cautious steps, they ventured forward. The air was thick with the smell of oil and rust.

In a dark corner, they finally found the reindeer. But it wasn't the cool high-tech creature they knew.

"Someone has taken it apart!" Leon said, shocked.

The reindeer's head, with its massive antlers, lay disconnected, its once-glowing eyes now dark and lifeless. The boys stared at the sad sight, their faces pale in the dim light.

Noah reached out, his fingers brushing against the cold metal of the reindeer's head. "Who would do such a thing?" he whispered.

Before Leon could open his mouth, footsteps echoed through the hall. The sound grew louder, amplified by the metal walls.

"Hide, quick!" Leon hissed.

They hastily ducked behind the remains of the reindeer. The footsteps grew closer, and against the dim light from the other end of the warehouse, they saw an ominous shadow that crawled toward them.

6
INGENIOUS CONSTRUCTORS

Noah peeked through a gap between the reindeer parts. The figure was slim and nimble, navigating the dark warehouse as if familiar with every shadowy corner.

"It's the guy from the market!" Leon whispered.

The figure halted, standing rigid as a statue, as if sensing that something was off.

Noah and Leon exchanged a nervous glance and held their breath, afraid that even the slightest exhale would give them away.

The figure moved towards the disassembled head of the reindeer, kneeling to examine it. For a heartbeat, Noah thought they were about to be discovered.

A buzzing sound broke the tension. The figure swiftly pulled out a cellphone and answered a call.

The conversation was in a language neither Noah nor Leon could understand, but the urgency in his voice was unmistakable. Over and over, he said a word that sounded like *"millions."*

"Why does he keep saying *millions*?" Leon whispered, with apprehension.

"I don't know," Noah replied, his thoughts spinning quickly. "But it seems like a lot of money is involved."

The man walked back and forth while talking on the phone.

Leon's eyes darted around, landing on a stack of wooden crates. He nudged Noah, pointing subtly. "What if we...you know, make a quick exit?"

Noah followed Leon's gaze. "You mean a sleigh?"

Leon nodded. "Remember the long slope just outside. We could slide right out of here!"

Noah's thoughts went into high gear as he caught on to Leon's plan. "Alright, but we need to be quick. He could end his call any moment now."

When the man turned his back on them, Noah and Leon swiftly yet silently began constructing their escape vehicle. Noah flipped a crate upside down and placed it on a discarded piece of tarp. "This should give us a smoother slide," he whispered.

Spotting a box cutter and what was left from a coiled rope nearby, Leon quickly used the cutter to snip off a length of rope. He then used it to secure the crate to the tarp by tying knots at each corner. "This should keep everything in place," he said, giving the knots an extra tug.

Using the last length of the rope, Noah securely tied the reindeer head to the front of the crate. "This will be our handle," he whispered back, giving it a tug to make sure it was firmly bound. "And it can serve as evidence later."

For the finishing touch, Leon wrapped his scarf around the crate, creating a pull rope. "I hope this holds," he whispered, gripping the scarf's ends tightly.

Noah nodded and positioned himself at the back. "On three," he said, determination in his eyes. "One... Two..."

Before he could say three, there was a jingling sound from Leon's pocket. With a clatter, the Christmas bells he had bought for his mom tumbled out, scattering across the floor.

The hooded figure quickly turned his head in their direction.

"Three!" Noah yelled.

With Leon pulling and Noah pushing from behind, they manoeuvred the sleigh towards the exit with all their strength.

7
THE GREAT SLEIGH ESCAPE

The hooded man shouted something incomprehensible. Then he sprinted towards the boys and lunged to grab Noah's leg. He tripped over the jingling Christmas bells and narrowly missed, crashing to the ground.

The boys felt the rush of cool morning air as they burst out of the warehouse, the sunlight momentarily blinding them. With the slope at their feet, they hopped onto their makeshift sleigh, allowing gravity to do the rest.

The sleigh picked up speed, the wind rushing past them, the ground a blur beneath. They raced into the forest, the thief's furious shouts fading into the wind. Soon, the trees surrounded them, with the warehouse and the thief out of sight.

With the slope leveling out, the sleigh gradually came to a gentle halt. The boys, their breaths heavy and faces flushed from the adrenaline, jumped off.

Leon chuckled, brushing glistening snowflakes off his cheek. "That was intense! Best sleigh ride ever!"

Noah nodded, still catching his breath. "Unforgettable for sure, but... where exactly are we?"

The surrounding dense forest painted a picture of serene solitude, with tall, snow-capped trees blocking out most of the winter sun. The only sounds were distant bird chirps and their own breathing.

"Feels like we're miles away from town," Leon observed, gazing at the vast expanse of trees.

Suddenly, the familiar pack of dogs emerged, wagging their tails and circling them.

"Look who's back!" Leon laughed. "Guess they've taken a liking to us!"

Noah, remembering the silhouette from the river, whispered, "I think... Frostbite might be guiding them, and us in turn."

Leon smirked, "Or they just want to hear the jingling bells again. Sorry, guys, they're gone!" He sighed. "And now I'm broke with no present for Mom."

The dogs began trotting in a particular direction, occasionally glancing back.

"Ok, let's follow them again", Noah said.

Guided by the dogs, the boys wove through the forest. Soon, patches of sunlight streamed through, warming their faces. The distant hum of city life became clearer with every step.

"You think these dogs are leading us back to town?" Leon wondered aloud.

"It seems so," Noah replied. "Look, up ahead. The trees are thinning out."

As they reached the edge of the forest, the dogs bounded off, disappearing into the wild.

Leon laughed in disbelief. "Can't believe we were so close to town the whole time!"

Their attention was caught by a quaint toy shop nestled between two buildings. A beautifully carved wooden sign swung gently in the breeze, reading *Mrs. Smith's Enchanted Emporium.*

Noah rested his hand on the cold metal of the reindeer head, gazing in the direction where the dogs had vanished. "There must be a reason they led us here."

With determination in their eyes and the reindeer head in tow, the boys pushed open the door to the toy store.

8
MRS. SMITH

With a soft jingle, the doorbell announced their arrival. Noah and Leon found themselves in a paradise teeming with whimsical toys. Miniature trains zoomed over floating tracks as if by magic. Wind-up robots and dolls chatted amongst themselves. A butterfly drone fluttered around the room.

At a workbench, they saw an older lady with white hair tinkering with a small mechanical bird. When she looked up, her eyes twinkled.

"Ah, my young adventurers!" she exclaimed, her face lighting up with a warm smile. Her British accent made her appear like a grandmother from an age-old fairy tale.

"You must be Mrs. Smith," Noah said, recalling the name they'd seen on the store's sign.

"Indeed, I am," she replied. "You look like you could use some help."

"Do we?" Leon asked, a shy smile creeping across his face.

Mrs. Smith's laughter was genuine. "Oh, my dear boy, a toy

merchant knows many things. Especially when two young lads waltz in with the head of a robotic reindeer!"

The boys exchanged awkward glances. Indeed, the robo-skull wasn't exactly a subtle thing to bring along.

Leon cleared his throat. "You see, Mrs. Smith, we believe the reindeer was stolen. We found this reindeer head in a rather...peculiar place. We escaped from the warehouse and then a pack of wild dogs led us here."

"A pack of wild dogs, you say?" Mrs. Smith peered over her reading glasses with interest.

"Yeah, I think Frostbite might have been leading them," Noah chipped in eagerly, "the guardian dog from the Christmas market legend."

He leaned forward, reciting.

"In winter's chill, at day or night,
Frostbite prowls, staying out of sight..."

Mrs. Smith raised an eyebrow, a knowing smile playing on her lips.

"If your heart is pure and your cause is right,
He'll guide you safely through the fright."

The boys looked at each other, amazed.

"You know the legend, too?" Leon asked.

Mrs. Smith laughed softly. "Ah, it's a tale as old as time. Passed down from generation to generation. Now, let's get back to this fascinating piece of technology, shall we?"

They placed the reindeer's head before her. With nimble fingers and a discerning eye, she examined its intricate mechanics.

"This isn't some run-of-the-mill robot," she muttered. "This is custom-built. Definitely not from around here."

Noah leaned in closer, his eyes narrowed with curiosity and constantly shifting between the reindeer head and Mrs. Smith. "Then where is it from?" he finally asked.

Mrs. Smith winked at him. "Ah, that's the thrilling question, isn't it? Let me look into it. In the meantime, feel free to explore. You might find something that tickles your fancy. Oh, and don't you worry, I'll inform the police that the reindeer was stolen from the market. Maybe they can confiscate the remaining parts at the warehouse."

Leon's eyes were drawn to the butterfly drone, its wings shimmering. Mrs. Smith laughed and handed him a smartphone to control it.

"Amazing!" Leon exclaimed, delighted as he maneuvered the drone through the air.

Time flew by, and eventually Mrs. Smith called them over. "I think I've discovered something, but I need a little more time. Can you leave the head here overnight?"

"Of course," Noah agreed, trusting her.

"Excellent," she said, pleased. "Come back tomorrow, and I'll have more to share."

9
INTERROGATION AT THE CHRISTMAS MARKET

"We should go back to Mr. Kruger," Noah declared. "He has to know more about the reindeer's origin."

They found the market manager in his tiny wooden cabin, surrounded by paperwork and layout plans for the market.

"You again," he grumbled dismissively, not bothering to look up from the stack of paperwork in front of him. "What do you want now?"

"We have more questions about the reindeer," Leon said, cutting straight to the chase.

Mr. Kruger sighed, finally lifting his gaze from the forms. His eyes met Leon's, and for a moment, they flickered with unease. "I told you, the reindeer was sent for repairs. That's it!"

The two boys exchanged a knowing glance.

Noah decided to play his cards close to his chest. "Where did it come from?" he asked, feigning innocence. "Who made it?"

Clearly annoyed and reddening in the face, Mr. Kruger

snapped, "That's none of your business." He paused and gripped the edge of his cluttered desk, as if steadying himself. "It was a gift."

"A gift?" Leon looked puzzled. "From whom?"

For a moment, Mr. Kruger hesitated, his lips pressed into a thin line. Out of the corner of his eye, he glanced at a small globe on his desk.

"From a foreign delegation," he finally said, spinning the globe absentmindedly. "They wanted to add some international touch to our market."

"What's a delegation?" Leon whispered to Noah.

"A group of important people," Noah explained. Then he leaned forward, looking Mr. Mr. Kruger straight in the eyes. "Which country did the delegation come from?"

Mr. Kruger halted the spinning globe with his finger. "That's none of your concern! Now leave me alone. I've got work to do!"

Noah put his hands flat on the table, trying to get a closer look at the globe. "We just want to know where the reindeer came from. It could give us clues as to why it was stolen."

Mr. Kruger seemed to pale for a moment. "Stolen? How do you know—" He then caught himself, his expression hardening. "That's it! Out with you!"

He stood up, hustled them out of the cabin, and slammed the door behind them.

The friends returned to the bustling Christmas market, weaving through the crowd of shoppers and families.

"He's definitely hiding something," Noah mused. "He clearly knows where the delegation's from."

Leon's eyes landed on the empty spot where the reindeer had been. "Without the reindeer, there's something missing," he said thoughtfully.

Noah looked at a stall that sold trinkets, including miniature igloos and polar bears. "We should dig deeper. Let's head over to the local library. Maybe we'll find answers there."

10
THE CONNECTION TO THE NORTH POLE

Noah and Leon stepped into the city library. "We need to find out more about this foreign delegation," Noah said, his eyes scanning the endless rows of books. "If the reindeer was a gift from another country, there have to be clues."

Leon was already deep in research on one of the library computers. "I found something about a delegation from Svalcadia! They were here a month ago."

Noah's brows furrowed. "Svalcadia? I've never heard of that place. Where is it?"

Leon continued scrolling on the computer. "It says here that Svalcadia is a small country near the North Pole. Sounds like a winter wonderland."

Noah's eyes lit up. "You know what? When Mr. Kruger stopped the spinning globe, his finger lingered near the North Pole. Maybe that's not a coincidence."

For hours, they immersed themselves in books and articles, captivated by the icy landscapes and the culture of Svalcadia. One topic, however, stood out: the robotics technology there.

"Check this out, Leon!" Noah pointed to an article about a futuristic robotics facility in Svalcadia. "Some of the world's most advanced robots are developed there. Maybe our reindeer came from that place!"

Surrounded by the gentle hum of library computers and the scent of old books, they delved into their research, losing track of time.

Leon even stumbled upon a photo of the visit from Svalcadia. "Noah, look!" He pointed to the screen. "The ambassador from Svalcadia, Mr. Magnus Eriksen, was part of the delegation!"

Noah leaned toward the screen and squinted, but the photo was too small to make out any details.

As the library's closing time approached, they gathered their materials. "We have a lot to think about," Noah muttered.

Leon nodded excitedly. "We're closing in on the heart of this mystery, Noah. I can sense it."

11
ALLURING TOYS

After their research at the library, Noah and Leon strolled through the streets towards the Christmas market. A poster in front of a store caught their eyes.

Noah read aloud, *"The Gift Your Child Really Wants!"*

Leon pulled his friend closer. "Hey, those toy reindeer look just like the robo-reindeer!" He pointed at the toy company's logo. "It's the same as the one on the flyer dropped by the thief when we bumped into him!"

As they stared at the poster, the reindeer's eyes, a piercing blue, seemed to glow and draw them in. Everything around them became fuzzy, like they were stepping into a different world.

"Noah, don't you want one too?" Leon finally asked, his voice barely above a whisper and tinged with an eerie compulsion.

Equally entranced, Noah nodded. "Yeah, I don't know why, but we absolutely need one."

The poster seemed to attract them magnetically, almost as if it wanted to swallow them both.

"We have to break free from it!" hissed Noah, tugging at Leon's arm.

"I can't look away! It's like it's got a hold on me!" Leon muttered, his eyes glued to the poster.

A chilling sensation snapped them back to reality—the feeling that they were being watched.

Noah looked around frantically. He saw only happy people walking through the snow. No one seemed to share their unease.

"Let's move, Leon," Noah urged, his voice quivering with a mix of desire and fear. "Now!"

With a huge effort, they pulled their eyes away from the poster and walked on, every step a battle of wills. The feeling of being watched intensified. Had their investigation attracted unwanted attention?

Soon, they stumbled upon a brightly lit sales booth. The vendor, a portly man with a snow-white beard, strikingly resembled Santa Claus himself.

"Ho, ho, ho, boys!" he chuckled warmly. "You look like you could use some cotton candy. Here, it's on the house!" He handed each of them a fluffy treat.

"Thanks, Santa," said Leon, the tension easing from his shoulders. "Where can we get those cool toy reindeer?"

"They're an exclusive item here at the Christmas market," the vendor replied, his voice dropping an octave. "They're selling like hotcakes. More stock is expected soon, but for now, they're all sold out."

Noah, still feeling the strange allure from earlier, murmured, "We really need to get our hands on one."

As they left the booth, he couldn't shake off the feeling that Santa's gaze was following them.

Leon nudged Noah. "Hey, Earth to Noah! We've got bigger reindeer to fry, remember?"

Noah snapped out of his reverie, his eyes refocusing. "If the stolen reindeer is from Svalcadia, maybe we should contact their embassy and report the theft."

"Sounds like a great idea!" Leon exclaimed with renewed enthusiasm. "Let's make that our first order of business tomorrow."

12
SANTA'S REAL JOB

The morning light pierced through the trees as Noah and Leon approached the embassy of Svalcadia. The coat of arms at the entrance reflected the first rays of sunshine.

Leon rushed ahead and pressed the doorbell, which cheerfully played Jingle Bells.

Noah couldn't help but smile. "Even their doorbell is in the Christmas spirit!"

Leon chuckled but then sighed. "Yeah, and it's a nifty reminder that I am empty-handed for my mom after dropping my own jingling bells."

A secretary led them into a fancy reception area on the first floor. Icy landscapes, polar bears, and Northern Lights adorned the walls.

Behind a massive desk sat Ambassador Magnus Eriksen. His elegant suit somehow didn't seem to go well with his long white beard and round glasses.

"Ah, the young detectives!" Mr. Eriksen exclaimed cheerfully.

"I've been expecting you."

Noah raised an eyebrow. "You have?"

The ambassador winked. "Of course! By the way, did you enjoy the cotton candy yesterday?"

Leon's eyes popped open as he recognized him. "You were the Santa at the stall?"

"Ho, ho, ho!" Mr. Eriksen's laugh echoed throughout the room.

Noah felt it sounded a bit forced.

"Indeed, that was me," Mr. Eriksen affirmed. "Nice side gig, right? It also helps me keep tabs on what's going on outside. I like to stay informed, especially about matters concerning my homeland."

"We're here to report a theft," Noah began cautiously.

The ambassador grew serious. "I appreciate that. I'm aware of the theft. The police have searched the warehouse, but it's empty now."

"The rest of the reindeer is gone?" Leon asked incredulously.

"Yes, unfortunately." Mr. Eriksen sighed. "What do you know about the thief?"

The boys recounted their experiences over the last few days. Mr. Eriksen listened intently, occasionally nodding or interjecting a question.

When they finished, he leaned back thoughtfully. "Very good investigative work! Please keep me in the loop if you find out more about the thief."

Noah agreed. "Will do."

Mr. Eriksen extended his hand. "Very good."

As the two boys left the embassy, clouds now obscured the sun, and a chilly wind blew. The coat of arms at the entrance, which was gleaming when they arrived, now seemed to be smothered in shadow.

Leon pulled his jacket closer. "Was it this cold when we went in?"

Noah didn't answer. His eyes were drawn to a window on the first floor of the embassy, where a curtain twitched ever so slightly.

"Hey, we should check in with Mrs. Smith about the reindeer head," Leon suggested, breaking the silence.

Noah nodded, glad they had a plan. "Yeah, let's do that."

13
THE SECRET CHIP

Once again, Noah and Leon were greeted by the cheerful chime of a bell as they pushed open the door to Mrs. Smith's toy shop. All around them, little machines buzzed, clicked, and whirred.

In the midst of this chaos sat Mrs. Smith, her glasses perched on her nose, examining the reindeer's head under a large magnifying glass. She had further disassembled it for a closer look.

"Ah, my young sleuths!" she exclaimed in her unmistakable British accent. "You're right on time!"

Leon's eyes twinkled with curiosity. "Did you find out anything, Mrs. Smith?"

She beckoned them over and gently ran her fingers over a tiny chip she had extracted from the reindeer's head. "This, my dears, is no ordinary technology. I've never seen anything like it before."

Noah leaned in, intrigued. "And what exactly does this chip do?"

Mrs. Smith sighed. "I can't say for sure, but it collects and processes an enormous amount of data."

Leon's eyebrows shot up, his mouth forming a surprised 'O'. "What kind of data?"

"I have no idea," Mrs. Smith admitted. "Everything is encrypted. It's beyond even my capabilities."

Leon pondered for a moment. "Maybe we should tell Ambassador Eriksen about this."

Noah nodded in agreement and dialed Mr. Eriksen's number.

After a brief wait, the ambassador's deep voice came through. "Noah! What brings me the honor?"

After Noah filled him in on their discovery, Mr. Eriksen cleared his throat. "Yes, that's correct. Chips are embedded throughout the reindeer. They serve to study climate change."

"Study climate change?" Noah pressed.

"Yes, it's a pioneering project from Svalcadia." Mr. Eriksen's voice brimmed with pride. "With the reindeer, we collect data on temperature, air quality, and other crucial information."

Leon let out a soft whistle. "So, the reindeer is like a superhero for the climate?"

Mr. Eriksen chuckled. "Yes, you could say that. That's why it's crucial we get the technology back."

Noah hesitated for a moment and then asked, "Do you want the reindeer's head back, Mr. Ambassador?"

Mr. Eriksen paused before answering, "For now, the chip will suffice. I'll send someone to pick it up."

Having overheard the conversation, Mrs. Smith chimed in, "Why hide such noble technology in a reindeer?"

Mr. Eriksen's tone turned serious. "Espionage. Not everyone cares about climate change. There are global interests that want to steal this technology for harmful purposes."

A frown creased Noah's forehead. "So, you've kept the project a secret?"

"That's exactly right," Mr. Eriksen confirmed.

After the call ended, everyone remained silent for a moment.

Breaking the silence, Leon wondered, "Do you have any of those toy reindeer here?"

"No, I don't have them." Mrs. Smith waved a hand dismissively, glancing at her carefully curated shelves. "I've seen those adverts, but they're only sold at the Christmas market, as far as I know."

Noah checked the time on his smartphone. "We should head back, Leon. And we need to figure out our next steps."

"All right," Leon agreed. "Thanks, Mrs. Smith. We'll be back."

14
A PLAN TAKES SHAPE

Noah sat in his room, the soft light of a desk lamp casting a glow on the photos, documents and scribbled notes spread out before him. His eyes darted between the pages as he tried to connect the dots.

Leon burst into the room, a toy moose in hand, gleefully prancing around as if mimicking the Robo-Reindeer. "Do you think someone would pay ransom for this guy?" he asked, holding up the toy.

Noah chuckled, amused by his friend's antics. "Not for the moose, Leon. It's what's inside that counts. The tech in that reindeer is something really special."

"Yeah, I know." Leon flopped down into his usual spot—a plush bean bag near Noah's bookshelf. "Something superhero-level special!"

Noah let out a brief laugh. "Exactly. If the ambassador is right, then that reindeer is more than just a holiday decoration. It could help our planet."

Leon furrowed his brow, setting the toy moose atop a stack of astronomy books. "Then why would someone want to steal it?"

Leaning back, Noah pondered the situation, his fingers interlocked behind his head. "Remember what the thief kept saying on the phone? Something about *millions*."

Leon picked up a miniature figurine from the shelf, pretending it was the thief. "So he's planning to sell it?"

"Probably," Noah affirmed, his gaze locking onto the figurine. "And anyone willing to pay millions for it likely has big plans."

Leon bit his lip. "Big and maybe...not good?"

Noah nodded solemnly. "That's what I'm afraid of. We can't let this technology fall into the wrong hands."

After a brief silence, Leon clenched his fist and declared, "We have to catch the thief, Noah. Before he sells the reindeer."

Sitting up, Noah's eyes shone with resolve. "Exactly, Leon. We need a plan."

Ideas flowed quickly, ranging from the absurd to the ingenious. Leon even suggested that they could dress up as elves to blend in at the market.

All of a sudden, Leon jumped up, grabbing the toy moose. "And what if we build a fake reindeer and place it where the real one was?"

He set the moose down on Noah's notes on the desk, then maneuvered the thief figurine toward it. "Maybe the thief will come back for seconds! And then..." He resolutely snatched the figurine with his other hand.

Noah's eyes lit up, his face breaking into a grin. "That's brilliant, Leon! And I know someone who can help us with that."

15
THE DECOY REINDEER

The morning after their brainstorming, Noah and Leon hustled to Mrs. Smith's toy store. Their steps were brisk, and their minds focused on one thing only: the decoy reindeer.

Mrs. Smith, engrossed in stitching up a teddy bear's torn paw, looked up curiously. "A reindeer decoy?" she repeated, peering over her glasses. "And you want to use it as bait?"

Leon nodded. "Yep, it just has to look as real as the original. Then he'll surely bite!"

Mrs. Smith set down her needle and thread and leaned back in her chair. She tapped her chin thoughtfully, weighing the feasibility of the idea. "For the body, we can use materials from the store. But for the head..." She left the sentence hanging.

Noah eagerly filled in the gaps. "We still have the head of the original reindeer which is exactly what the thief is missing!"

Mrs. Smith clapped her hands enthusiastically. "Brilliant! That will make our bait perfect!"

The cozy toy store transformed into a bustling inventor's workshop. Mrs. Smith rummaged through shelves, gathering old toy parts, blueprints, and even fur from a retired teddy bear. The trio worked tirelessly.

Mrs. Smith even took it up a notch. She tinkered with a tiny circuit board, then nestled it into the reindeer's flank. "This little device will set off an alarm as soon as anyone tampers with our reindeer," she declared with a triumphant smile.

By the time the afternoon sun was pouring through the shop's windows, they stepped back to admire their work. The decoy was almost challenging anyone to distinguish it from the original.

Leon jumped, clapping his hands. "This is beyond awesome!"

The next step was to get Mr. Kruger, the market manager, on board. The boys approached him with a bit of apprehension; his earlier behaviour had left them puzzled.

But to their surprise, he was instantly on board. "If it helps catch this thief..." Mr. Kruger adjusted his glasses and nodded. "The reindeer was our showpiece, after all!"

Soon enough, the reindeer was the center of attention in the marketplace. Noah, Leon, Mrs. Smith, and even Mr. Kruger hid nearby.

To lighten the tense atmosphere, Leon whispered, "What if the reindeer takes off?"

Noah chuckled. "With Mrs. Smith's tech, I wouldn't even be surprised!"

16
MIDNIGHT

The Christmas market was abandoned and empty. The only light came from the moon above. Hours had passed, and the cold was creeping into everyone's bones.

"Are you sure we'll see this through, Leon?" Noah asked.

Leon shivered but looked resolute. "Bet we will," he said, determination in his voice.

From their hiding spot behind a Christmas tree, the boys, Mrs. Smith, and Mr. Kruger watched the area around the decoy reindeer. Tension crackled in the air. Every rustle, every faint noise had them snapping their heads.

Then, as the clock tower struck midnight, a figure emerged from the shadows and stealthily approached the reindeer.

"Noah," Leon whispered, his voice barely rising above the wind, "that's him!"

The thief swung onto the reindeer with a graceful motion. Noah and Leon exchanged glances, their hearts pounding.

"He thinks he can ride it away again!" Leon whispered.

A loud honk shattered the silence, followed by a blinding flash of light. Mrs. Smith's alarm had worked.

"Gotcha!" Leon shouted, leaping courageously from his hiding spot.

Temporarily blinded, the thief lost his balance, tumbled off the reindeer, and knocked it over in a clatter of metal.

"You thought you could catch me that easily?" he sneered, picking himself up.

Noah stepped out into the dim moonlight, mustering his courage. "What's so important about this reindeer that you'd risk so much?"

The thief laughed—a cold, mocking laugh. "The reindeer? It's nothing but a hollow shell without the chip. With the chip, though..." He paused and seemed to savor the moment. "It's a goldmine."

Without another word, the thief burst into a sprint, almost toppling a stack of crates in his haste.

"After him!" Leon shouted.

The thief deftly weaved between the stalls, gaining ground.

The boys sprinted after him, followed by Mrs. Smith and Mr. Kruger. The chase led from the market to the town center. The echo of their footsteps reverberated through the empty alleys.

But the thief was agile. Mrs. Smith and Mr. Kruger soon couldn't keep up with the frenetic pace and fell behind.

Gasping for air, Noah and Leon felt their energy waning.

"We need a shortcut!" Leon panted.

An idea flashed through Noah's mind. "This way!" he yelled, pulling Leon into an old cobblestoned passageway.

They weaved through the narrow alley, their breaths echoing

off the stone walls.

As they rounded a corner, they found themselves face to face with the thief.

17
MOONLIGHT CHASE

"Stop!" Leon yelled.

Ignoring the command, the thief vanished into a side street, the boys hot on his heels.

"We can't let him get away!" Leon shouted.

The thief zigzagged through the narrow lanes, attempting to lose them. Finally, he darted into a dead-end alley. Without hesitation, he began to scale a wall, agile as a weasel, making use of pipes and protrusions.

Leon tried to mimic him but slipped, unable to get a grip on the cold, wet bricks. "He's getting away!" he exclaimed, frustrated.

Noah stood behind Leon, looking up. Beyond the thief scaling the wall, the moon shone brightly.

Frostbite prowls, staying out of sight…

A loud noise pierced through the night. For Noah, it seemed like a mystical bark emanating from nowhere and everywhere simultaneously.

The thief was distracted for a moment. He lost his footing and slid down, landing headfirst in a pile of snow.

"Good job, Frostbite!" Noah cheered.

Finally, Mrs. Smith and Mr. Kruger caught up with them, panting.

"What the Dickens is going on?" Mrs. Smith asked, wiping her forehead.

"You should've seen it, Mrs. Smith!" Noah exclaimed, pointing his finger up the wall. "The thief got halfway up there, when Frostbite's bark distracted him!"

Mr. Kruger laughed. "Frostbite? That's just an old legend. You kids have such vivid imaginations!"

Leon turned to Noah and whispered, "To be honest, to me it sounded more like the engine of a starting car."

Noah scanned the area but saw no sign of Frostbite. Had he imagined it? He wasn't sure.

His gaze finally landed on the thief, who was groaning in the snow. "Okay, I give up!" he whined.

Noah took a step closer. "Who would be willing to pay millions for a reindeer chip?"

The thief looked up and offered a shaky grin. "You wouldn't believe it...."

Before he could say more, they were blinded by headlights. A limousine pulled up, and out stepped Ambassador Eriksen.

"Let's leave the questioning to the professionals, shall we?" Mr. Eriksen boomed, his voice brooking no room for argument.

Mrs. Smith looked at him in surprise. "Mr. Ambassador, what brings you here at this hour?"

"This is a matter of utmost importance to my homeland," Mr. Eriksen said, his mouth twisting into a crooked smile. "Kruger, cuff him!" he commanded, his voice as cold as the night air.

Mr. Kruger dug into his overcoat, the glint of metal catching the moonlight as he pulled out a pair of handcuffs. With a smirk, he clicked them securely around the thief's wrists.

"Comfortable?" Mr. Kruger mocked, yanking the thief to his feet.

"As a feather!" the thief shot back.

With a forceful nudge, Mr. Kruger led the thief to the limousine and shoved him inside. Mr. Eriksen climbed in after him, settling onto the plush leather with a satisfied sigh before pulling the door closed.

Rolling down the window just a bit, Mr. Eriksen looked out. "Your assistance is appreciated. Rest assured, he'll be handed over to the proper authorities."

The window rolled back up as the limo roared to life and sped off, leaving tire tracks in the snow.

After the car had turned a corner and disappeared, Noah and Leon exchanged a glance.

"Operation Reindeer Rescue: mission accomplished!" Leon eventually declared, with a mix of relief and pride.

"Yeah," Noah replied, "but something's not adding up. Who wanted to buy the tech from the thief?"

Mrs. Smith furrowed her brow as she wiped a stray snowflake from her cheek. "Since when does Mr. Kruger work for the embassy? It seems a little odd to me."

Her eyes met those of the boys, and a silent understanding passed between them. Whatever was happening, it was not over.

"Come on, let's go home. It's cold, and it's way past midnight," Mrs. Smith finally said.

18
AN INVITATION FROM THE NORTH

News of Noah and Leon's heroic efforts to catch the reindeer thief spread like wildfire. The local paper had blown up the story, and wherever the boys went, they were met with applause and appreciative pats on the back.

Amid the celebrations, Mrs. Smith called them into her toy store. The old bell jingled as they walked in.

Mrs. Smith, with a sly smile on her face, handed them a lovingly wrapped package. "For the bravest boys in town," she said, winking at them.

Leon eagerly tore off the gift wrap, revealing a miniature drone. "The butterfly drone!" he exclaimed, his eyes lighting up with delight.

Mrs. Smith laughed. "I thought you two deserved a little reward for all your hard work."

Noah smiled until his cheeks hurt. "Thank you, Mrs. Smith. We promise to take good care of it."

But the day had another surprise in store for them. When they got home, an official letter sealed with the emblem of Svalcadia awaited them.

Dear Noah and Leon,

In recognition of your efforts and sharp minds, I, Ambassador Magnus Eriksen, officially invite you for a visit to Svalcadia.

Your bravery has not only touched the hearts of your fellow citizens but has also reached the icy shores of my homeland.

I believe it's only fair and just for you to experience firsthand the land from which the technological marvel you so passionately protected hails.

Please consider this as a token of Svalcadia's gratitude.

Yours sincerely,
Magnus Eriksen
Ambassador

Noah read the letter aloud, and both boys were beside themselves with excitement. The thought of visiting Svalcadia made their hearts soar.

"We'll get to see where the reindeer comes from!" Leon exclaimed.

Noah nodded in anticipation. "Svalcadia, here we come!"

19
THE ROBOTICS FACTORY

The plane started its descent, and Noah and Leon gazed down at the icy landscapes of Svalcadia. Glaciers and mountains offered a breathtaking view.

"Wow, Noah, we're in a winter wonderland!" exclaimed Leon, his nose squished against the window.

Noah's mom, who had tagged along, handed them sandwiches. "Isn't it marvelous?" She smiled, pleased to see the boys' excitement.

On the ground, Ambassador Eriksen greeted them.

"Welcome to Svalcadia!" he announced grandly. "We have immense natural beauty and cutting-edge technology. Prepare to be amazed!"

They arrived at an ultra-advanced robotics factory. The building was sleek and modern, seeming almost out of place amidst the rugged natural beauty.

"I'll let you boys enjoy the robotics tour," Noah's mom said as they approached the factory. "Technology isn't really my cup of tea, so I'll wait for you in the cafeteria. I've heard they have excellent cocoa here." She winked.

Inside, the factory was warm, the air sterile, and the atmosphere buzzing with the hum of machinery. Robotic arms, conveyor belts, and workstations filled the massive space. "This is where the magic happens," said Mr. Eriksen, his eyes sparkling with pride.

The boys watched as robots wheeled around, assembling parts or checking quality. Engineers scurried about like busy ants amidst the machinery.

Leon pointed at a robot gracefully dancing. "It moves just like a human!"

Mr. Eriksen chuckled. "Ah, that's our latest project. We're trying to build robots that mimic human movements."

He pressed a button, and the robot transitioned smoothly from a waltz to a tango, its mechanical limbs moving with an eerie fluidity.

As Noah admired the robot's intricate dance steps, his foot caught on an oddly elevated section of the floor.

Absorbed in his explanation, Mr. Eriksen continued, "We've integrated thousands of sensors to capture the essence of human motion." He paused and smirked. "And if they dance well enough, we invite them to our next party! "

Noah noticed that the edges of the elevated section looked out of place. It seemed to subtly ripple. When he looked closer, he saw that it was a trapdoor.

While they continued their tour, he nudged Leon and subtly pointed it out. Leon's eyes widened, but before they could investigate further, a commotion erupted. A small robotic dog had gone rogue, chasing its own tail.

As engineers scrambled to contain the chaos, Mr. Eriksen laughed. "Not all our experiments are successful."

Seizing the moment, Leon pulled out his phone. "Mr. Eriksen, could you pose with the rogue dog? Mrs. Smith would love this!"

Mr. Eriksen chuckled and obliged.

The dog zigzagged between everyone's legs, causing one engineer to trip and another to spill a box of screws.

"Got everything on video!" Leon exclaimed. Then he tapped his phone a few times, looking puzzled. "Hey, why isn't it sending?"

Noah leaned in and whispered, "Remember, we're in a foreign country. Our phones don't have roaming, so we can't send messages or make calls."

"Ah, right." Leon sighed. "I'll show her when we get back."

Mr. Eriksen cleared his throat. "Now, let me show you how we cherish failure in this factory. We believe that every mistake is a step toward success."

He led them to a wall filled with photos, blueprints, and even some charred robot parts. "This is our Hall of Oops."

He pointed to a photo of a robot covered in foam. "This one misinterpreted 'put out the fire' and sprayed foam all over the lab."

"A bubble bath straight from a robot's dream!" Leon quipped.

Mr. Eriksen gestured to another photo. "This one was supposed to predict your needs before you articulate them—"

Noah interrupted, a strange sensation creeping over him. "You mean like a mind-reading robot?"

"Well, not exactly," Mr. Eriksen clarified. "I aimed the machine to predict simple choices, like the card you'd pick from a deck. But all it managed to do was guess that the lab assistant wanted coffee. Which, between you and me, anyone could have predicted at nine a.m. on a Monday."

Leon made a face. "Maybe the robot needs some coffee to make better predictions!"

"I've shelved that project for now," Mr. Eriksen added, steering the tour to its end. "I am focusing on more, shall we say, practical applications."

As they approached the cafeteria for a break, Noah's mom rejoined them, handing out some snacks. "You boys look like you could use a pick-me-up."

Noah whispered to Leon, "We need to find out what's up with that trapdoor."

20
WHISPERS IN THE WIND

After the tour concluded, Ambassador Eriksen's phone rang. "Excuse me for a moment," he muttered, disappearing through the factory's front entrance.

Noah's mom approached the boys. "Would you like some hot chocolate?"

"Thanks, but we'll get some fresh air," Noah replied.

Noah's mom looked concerned. "It's freezing out there. Make sure you put on your jackets and scarves."

"Thanks, Mom. We'll be okay," Noah assured her.

Bundled up in multiple layers, hats, and gloves, the boys stepped outside. Svalcadia's notorious cold was living up to its reputation. The icy wind bit into their cheeks, penetrating their thick clothing and making them shiver.

From a distance, they saw Mr. Eriksen pacing back and forth, deeply involved in his conversation.

"Come on!" Noah hissed, pulling Leon behind a snowdrift. The wind carried snippets of words their way.

Mr. Eriksen's boots crunched the snow as he paced, his voice laced with amusement. "...boys...completely in the dark..." He kicked at a pile of snow, scattering it into the wind. "Reindeer technology... Climate change!" He erupted in hearty laughter.

Leon tugged at Noah's jacket. "Why is he laughing so hard?"

Mr. Eriksen's voice grew softer, almost swallowed by the wind's whistle. "Imagine, if we could make every child..."

Just as they strained to catch the next words from his lips, a concerned voice broke through the wind. "You'll catch a cold!"

Both boys jumped. Turning around, they saw Noah's mom approaching, holding a steaming cup of hot chocolate in each hand.

"Oh, uh, thanks," stammered Noah, casting a surreptitious glance toward Eriksen, who was still absorbed in his talk.

Noah's mom gestured them to follow her back into the factory. "Come on, you've been outside long enough."

They returned inside, taking sips from their cups. The warmth filled their bodies but only partly distracted them from their chilling questions.

"Noah," Leon whispered, lowering his cup, "what the heck are they planning with that reindeer technology?"

"I have a feeling it's something less funny than a robo-dog chasing its tail," Noah replied, setting his cup down on the cafeteria's counter. "But we're going to find out."

In the evening, after Mr. Eriksen had shown them around an ice cave, he dropped them off at the hotel with a wink. "More of Svalcadia to explore tomorrow," he promised.

However, instead of sinking into the plush comfort of their hotel beds, Noah and Leon snuck out, their hearts pounding with excitement.

The night sky was painted with shades of green and pink like in a fairy tale. The factory building loomed ahead.

21
BENEATH THE TRAPDOOR

Leon pressed his back against the factory's icy wall. "Noah, how are we going to get in there?"

Noah looked at Leon, his eyes resolute. "Don't worry. I took care of it."

Leon's eyes widened. "What? When?"

Noah leaned in closer, lowering his voice. "Remember when that robotic dog went nuts, chasing its own tail?"

Leon nodded, recalling the chaos. "Yeah, that was hilarious!"

Noah continued, grinning. "Exactly. While everyone was distracted and you were capturing that video with Eriksen, I snuck away for a moment."

Leon's eyes widened in anticipation. "You did? And then?"

Noah chuckled. "I found a window nearby that wasn't bolted like the others. I unlatched it, just enough so that it could be opened later."

Leon shook his head in admiration. "You sly fox!"

Noah led Leon to the window, his eyes scanning for any signs of movement. "Ready?" he whispered.

Leon gulped. "As I'll ever be."

With a gentle push, the window creaked open just wide enough for them to slip through. They held their breath as they snuck inside, eyes darting to every shadow, every flicker of light.

Inside, the factory seemed to pulse like a sleeping beast waiting to be awakened. The low hum of dormant machinery filled the air, and lights blinked in a steady rhythm. Each of their footsteps resonated through the empty hallways.

After winding their way through the maze of corridors, they found themselves standing before the mysterious trapdoor. It creaked as they pried it open with combined effort.

A metal staircase led down into a storage room. The air was stale and musty.

"It looks like—" Noah began.

"A toy store straight out of a horror film!" Leon finished.

Rows of shelves were packed with small toy reindeer—hundreds, maybe thousands of them—all identical, all with the same hypnotic blue eyes.

"We've seen this before!" Leon exclaimed, pointing at a poster.

"*The Gift Your Child Really Wants!*" Noah read aloud.

Scattered across a table were papers and business plans.

Noah started flipping through them, his eyes scanning the pages, as Leon's phone flashlight shone over them. "These toys aren't just expensive; they're all the rage!"

Leon's hand shook slightly, causing the light to flicker. "Why is everyone buying them like crazy?"

Footsteps sounded. Louder, closer.

Eriksen's voice echoed through the corridors, mocking and triumphant. "Noah, Leon, you little master detectives! I had a feeling you'd show up here!"

Noah's heart pounded so loudly that he feared Eriksen might hear it. "We need to get out of here, now!" he whispered.

Their only exit was the trapdoor they'd come through, and Eriksen was closing in fast.

"You can't hide!" Eriksen's voice boomed, occupying the space, having almost reached the trapdoor.

"Up here!" Noah pointed to a ventilation shaft near the ceiling. "Quick, help me with the table!"

With adrenaline surging through their veins, they shoved the table across the concrete floor, its legs screeching. The documents that had been on the table scattered everywhere. With no time to choose, Noah grabbed random pages off the floor and shoved them hastily into his pocket.

They climbed on top of the table just as the trapdoor above the stairs slammed shut with a loud bang. Then, they heard the heavy thud of boots descending.

"Quick, get in!" Noah urged as he hoisted Leon into the shaft. Then he scrambled up himself.

"Where are you, boys?" Eriksen sneered maliciously from the bottom of the stairs.

The two crawled into the darkness, hearts racing, barely daring to breathe. The shaft was a tight fit, forcing them to hunch their shoulders and scrape their knees as they moved.

Behind them, they sensed more than saw the blue, glowing eyes of the toy reindeer.

Then they heard Eriksen's muffled voice reverberating through the shaft. "Don't worry, boys, I'll see you 'round!"

22
THE TRUE FACE

Navigating the dim light provided by Leon's phone flashlight, Noah and Leon crept forward. The space was tight, and they felt every bump and rivet in the cold metal beneath their hands and knees.

"Almost there," Noah whispered, catching a glimpse of a larger space ahead.

At the end of the shaft, they peered down into a massive storage room. Everywhere were shelves filled with mechanical parts: robot arms, legs, gears, and all sorts of robotic figures and unidentifiable gadgets.

"We have to get down there," Noah whispered.

Leon nodded in agreement.

They gripped the edge of the vent as they used cables from the shaft to carefully climb down. Just as their feet touched the ground, the storage room door creaked open. The towering silhouette of Ambassador Eriksen cast a long shadow into the room.

The boys ducked behind a shelf as the ambassador sauntered in, dressed in a red coat and matching Santa hat. His eyes, once friendly, now glittered dangerously.

"Boys, boys," he sang in a tone of mock friendliness, "you've done marvelously! You've saved me so much trouble."

"What does he mean?" Leon whispered to Noah.

"The money, the technology, the reindeer at the Christmas market...it's all connected," Noah murmured back.

Eriksen turned toward them. "You're absolutely right!" he exclaimed, having overheard Noah. "Want to know how?"

"You have secretly developed technology that can mess with thoughts," Noah answered, his voice filled with contempt he didn't bother to hide.

Eriksen let out a laugh, pausing to admire a robot's head. "Smart guy! The captivating blue eyes of your beloved market reindeer—remember? Anyone who looks long enough will feel an irresistible urge to buy my pricey toys."

"That's why we wanted one of those reindeer so badly," Leon whispered, full of regret.

Eriksen walked around, inspecting a robot arm here, tapping a gear there, as if contemplating their future utility.

"And there's more!" he continued, leaning against a table laden with robotic parts. "I've also incorporated this technology into the small toy reindeer. Once they're in a child's room, the little darlings will start desiring more and more expensive products."

"That's evil!" Leon exclaimed.

Eriksen shrugged, pushing away from the table. "Evil or just good business? Perspective, my dear boy."

Noah closed his eyes. Everything clicked into place. The fuss about protecting the climate had been a lie. Eriksen's scheme felt like a betrayal.

"Mr. Kruger makes sure my toys are sold at the Christmas market. Together we'll be unstoppable," Eriksen gloated.

"So Mr. Kruger is in on this too?" Leon whispered, his voice shaky.

"Of course! He gets a share of the profits." Eriksen grinned, fixing his gaze on the boys' hiding spot.

"What about the thief?" Noah asked, already guessing what the answer would be.

Eriksen scoffed. "Oh, he was a real pain," he admitted. "He wanted to sell the tech to the highest bidder. I was willing to shell out *millions* to get it back. But thanks to your clever trap, I didn't have to pay a dime."

Eriksen had used them. Noah felt rage building inside him, a determination to make things right. His cheeks flushed with anger, his fists clenched.

If your heart is pure and your cause is right...

Noah boldly stepped out from his hiding spot. "You won't get away with this!"

Eriksen's face twisted into a malicious smile. "Oh, I believe I already have, young man."

With that, he pressed a button on a remote, and the machinery in the room sprang to life. Arms swung, gears turned, and an army of robots began to advance toward Noah and Leon.

"By the way, thank you for accepting my invitation to Svalcadia," Eriksen yelled over the increasing roar of the machines. "That was the cleverest trap of all! Goodbye, boys."

23
THE ROBOT ARMY

After Eriksen had left the room, the machinery came alive. Dozens of glowing robot eyes activated, casting eerie red and blue lights that danced like malevolent fireflies in the room.

"Leon!" Noah yelled, attempting to be heard over the din of the gears and hydraulics. "The drone!"

Leon's eyes met Noah's, and he nodded. With shaky hands, he pulled out the butterfly drone Mrs. Smith had given them.

He activated the drone with his smartphone, and the tiny device zipped into the air, its wings fluttering like a living creature.

The robots appeared disoriented, their actions thrown off as their sensors tried to lock onto the fast-moving drone. Leon's fingers glided over the controls. He skillfully maneuvered the drone around the room, making it twirl, dive and spin.

The machines, entranced by the dance, seemed to forget their initial mission. They stumbled and crashed into each other like dancers in a botched ballet.

Sparks flew, metal claws broke, and gears jammed.

"Well done, Leon!" Noah yelled. "Let's get out of here!" He grabbed Leon's arm and pulled him toward the door.

Just as they reached it, Eriksen's imposing figure appeared, blocking their way. "Ho, ho, ho! Enough of this, you wannabe superheroes!"

Noah locked eyes with Eriksen, his gaze unyielding. "You underestimated us, Mr. Ambassador!" he retorted, his voice laden with defiance. "Two good friends with pure hearts can achieve a lot more than you think!"

"Pure hearts!" Eriksen roared with laughter, clutching his belly. "Who would ever believe you two? A couple of rascals against the venerable Ambassador Magnus Eriksen?"

Noah pulled out his phone and turned the screen toward Eriksen. "You might want to watch what you say, Mr. Ambassador," Noah said, his voice calm. "I've been recording every word you've said since you entered this room."

Eriksen's laughter died. It was replaced by a flash of disbelief, and then dawning realization. His eyes narrowed.

Seizing the moment of Eriksen's stunned silence, Leon reactivated the drone and steered it toward a light switch.

With precision, he nudged the drone to flip the switch, plunging the room into total darkness.

"Your game's up, Mr. Ambassador!" Leon exclaimed.

Before Eriksen could react, both boys slipped past him, jamming the door behind them to leave him locked in the dark.

Noah and Leon rushed back to the window they had entered through. Noah pushed it open, and both boys scrambled out, tumbling into the snow-covered ground outside.

Their hearts pounded wildly, but they were out.

"We need to call the police!" Leon gasped, pulling out his phone.

Then he stared at the screen in disbelief, his face pale as he looked up. "No service, Noah. Our phones don't work here, remember?"

Desperation gripped them. With no way to call for help, they were stuck.

24
THE FROSTENBITT MOMENT

Noah's breath fogged up in the icy air as he trudged through the snow, his mind racing as fast as his heart.

"What do we do now, Noah? We're stuck in Svalcadia without working phones!" Leon's voice trembled, partly from the cold and partly from desperation.

Noah looked up at the sky as if searching for an answer among the stars.

He'll guide you safely through the fright.

Noah paused, feeling a spark of inspiration light up his thoughts. "What if?" he muttered, his eyes glowing with an idea.

"What if what?" Leon said, coming to a halt.

Noah grabbed Leon's arm. "The village! We drove through it on the way to the ice cave. It's really close!"

"Right!" Leon agreed, his hope reignited. "They should have a police station, right?"

"We won't know until we try," Noah responded. With that, he

led Leon into a dash, heading in the direction they had driven earlier that day.

***

After what felt like an eternity of running through the icy wilderness, they reached the outskirts of the village. The boys' eyes widened at the sight of the town sign: *Welcome to Frostenbitt!*

"Talk about a guardian through the fright," Noah remarked, feeling a sense of ease.

Leon smirked. "Maybe Frostbite has a relative here. You know, maybe there's a grain of truth in that legend after all."

Signs pointed them past quaint wooden homes to the *Politistasjon*.

When they burst into the police station, a warm blast of air hit them. The cozy interior was a welcome relief from the biting cold.

"We need to speak to someone! It's urgent!" Noah panted.

A gruff officer looked up from his desk, his face as crinkled as a paper ball. "Slow down, kiddos. What's the emergency?"

A familiar voice interjected, "Noah? Leon?"

They turned to see Noah's mom, her face a mix of relief and concern.

"Mom! What are you doing here?" Noah exclaimed.

"I woke up and found both of you gone. I was so worried I reported you missing! What's going on?"

The boys spilled the beans—everything from Eriksen's scheme to the robotic factory to the toy reindeer that could mind-control kids.

The officer raised an eyebrow. "Ambassador Eriksen? You're accusing a high-ranking official. You expect me to believe all this?"

Noah reached into his pocket and pulled out the pages he'd grabbed. They were detailed business plans outlining Eriksen's scheme. Then he played back the recording on his phone.

Leon also whipped out his phone. "And let's not forget the butterfly drone with a built-in camera!"

He played the footage, which showed the robots going haywire and Eriksen boasting, "A couple of rascals against the venerable Ambassador Magnus Eriksen?" just before the recording went black.

The officer's eyes widened. "By the reindeer of Svalcadia, this is serious!"

They sped back to the factory with the police, sirens wailing.

As they entered the facility, the door to the storage room was still jammed shut. Inside, they found Eriksen, surrounded by his malfunctioning robot army.

Eriksen was faced with the evidence—secret documents, a recorded confession, incriminating drone footage, a destroyed robot army, and a room full of toy reindeer. He seemed to hesitate, as if contemplating one last grand lie. But then, he cracked.

"I did it, all right?" he sobbed. "I wanted to sell the reindeer, control the market, make millions!"

The officer, with a deadpan expression, slapped on the handcuffs. "Magnus Eriksen, you're under arrest for fraud, conspiracy, and making really creepy toys."

As Eriksen was led away, Noah's mom hugged both boys tightly. "I was so worried, but I should've known. You two always land on your feet."

"And sometimes on the snow," Leon quipped, earning a chuckle from everyone.

EPILOGUE
A CHRISTMAS TO REMEMBER

Noah and Leon returned to their hometown, arriving just in time for the grand finale of the Christmas market. The festive atmosphere hit them as they strolled toward the central square.

They stopped dead in their tracks. There, in a place of honor, stood their decoy reindeer—adorned with twinkling lights and a shiny red nose.

"Look who's the star of the show now," Leon said, nudging Noah.

"Our decoy's gone prime time." Noah chuckled in agreement.

They were interrupted by the buzz of a crowded nearby stall. Intrigued, they wove their way through the crowd to find a sign that read *Mrs. Smith's Enchanted Emporium*.

Wearing a shimmering shawl and a Santa hat, Mrs. Smith was busy attending to customers. Seeing the boys, her eyes sparkled. "Ah, my young heroes! Good to see you back in one piece!"

"Thanks, Mrs. Smith!" Leon laughed. "And your toys are causing quite the stir! Seems like the market has a new hit."

Mrs. Smith beamed. "Well, after that hypnotic reindeer debacle, Mr. Martinez asked if I'd fancy setting up a stall. He's the new market organizer and—"

"Wait, Mr. Martinez?" Noah interrupted, puzzled.

A familiar voice boomed from behind them, "That'd be me!"

The boys turned to find the security guard who had told them about the Frostbite legend a few days ago. A shiny new badge declared his title: Mr. Martinez, Market Organizer.

Leon's jaw dropped. "You're the new organizer? What happened to Mr. Kruger?"

Mr. Martinez chuckled. "Always had my suspicions about him. Glad you boys uncovered the truth. After his arrest, I was offered this position. And who better to set things right?"

Leon grinned. "Every place needs its guardian, huh?"

A flustered Mrs. Smith interrupted their reunion. "Boys, as much as I love our little natters, I'm up to my ears here! Can't keep up with the demand."

Noah smiled. "Need a hand, Mrs. Smith?"

"Hmm, can you promise not to set any traps this time?" she teased.

Swiftly, Noah and Leon sprang into action. Noah took up his post behind the counter, managing the inventory and handling transactions. He was in his element, organizing the chaos into a smooth operation.

Leon, meanwhile, became the entertainer, wowing the crowd with toy demonstrations. When he got to the butterfly drone, the atmosphere electrified.

With a wave of his hand, he sent it soaring into the air. It twirled, looped and danced, capturing the crowd's attention as effectively as it had confused Eriksen's robotic machinery. Gasps and cheers filled the air as Leon piloted the fluttering butterfly back to his palm with a flourish.

While observing the spectacle, Noah caught sight of two familiar faces in the crowd—his parents. He saw a blend of pride and wonder in their gaze. A few feet away, Leon's mom, usually so consumed by her work, stood watching her son captivate the crowd. Her eyes shimmered with unshed tears of joy.

The boys exchanged a quick, knowing glance. This was it—the real magic of Christmas. Not in grand adventures or expensive gifts like the jingling bells Leon had lost, but in the simple, heartfelt moments that brought people together.

As the evening drew to a close, the sky above the market square bloomed with fireworks, painting the night with hues of red, green, and gold.

Mrs. Smith, now able to catch her breath, joined the boys. "Seems like the market has found its spirit again, thanks to you two," she said, patting the boys on their heads.

Leon looked at Noah and then back at Mrs. Smith. "It was a team effort. Besides, we couldn't have done it without the help of the real-life Santa and her *Enchanted Emporium*," he said, smiling toward Mrs. Smith.

Noah chuckled. "Yeah, and not to forget a guardian who believes in legends."

"And two lads who believed in the goodness of hearts!" finished Mrs. Smith.

While the crowd was engrossed in the fireworks, Noah's gaze wandered.

In winter's chill, at day or night...

For a moment, he thought he saw the shadow of a large white dog lurking behind a deserted stall. But as a burst of a rocket illuminated the sky, he saw it was just smoke from the fireworks.

ABOUT THE AUTHOR

Amidst the beer gardens and pretzels of Munich, Germany, Sebastian spends most days knee-deep in legal briefs and courtroom drama.

Inspired to create a special Christmas surprise for his nephews, he put away his lawyer's gown and the memo he was working on to pen this modern Christmas tale.

IF YOU LIKED THIS BOOK...

...then please consider giving it a five-star review on Amazon!
Cheers. ☺

Printed in Great Britain
by Amazon